SINGING FOR EARTH TREES

唱和地球树

SHI BI

尸比 著

(IN CHINESE)

(中文)

Copyright © 2021 SHI BI

All rights reserved

权利保留

侵权必究

ISBN: 978-1-7378679-4-4

父母养育儿女

儿女提携父母

前言

笔名： 尸比

姓名： 史瑞芳

生日： 公元 1944 年 4 月 21 日（农历 3 月 29 日）

出生地： 生于中国四川宜宾市珙县，后随父又返蓉。

成长地： 之前，四川成都市西城区梵音寺街 48 号成长，念梵音寺小学；之后，重庆市江北区五里店红土地特 1 号字水中学教书。1970 年 5 月至 1999 年 5 月在重庆市字水中学工作，直到退休，教龄 30 年。

笔名典故： 在成都市二十六中（女子）初中时，身体爱打屁，有次有人叫我的绰号"屁炮"时，我就说，我以后发表文章用笔名就叫"尸比"。

目录

歌曲 1

1. 壹. 徒步缙云 1
2. 《徒步缙云》创作背景 2
3. 《徒步缙云》歌词 2
4. 《徒步缙云》原稿 3
5. 听《徒步缙云》有感【中文】 4
6. 听《徒步缙云》有感【中文原稿】 ... 5
7. 听《徒步缙云》有感【英文】 6
8. 听《徒步缙云》有感【英文原稿】 ... 8
9. 贰. 树桩 9
10. 《树桩》创作背景：唱和地球树 10
11. 《树桩》原稿 11

i

12. 咏《树桩》序 瑞芳 12

13. 咏《树桩》序 一陟 12

14. 《树桩》律诗与英文翻译 12

15. 《树桩》儿歌 瑞芳 13

16. 《树桩》七绝 一陟 13

17. 《枯木树桩赞》散文 同贵 14

18. 《树桩》修改历程 15

19. 叁. 昆华赠围巾 17

20. 《昆华赠围巾》原诗 18

和诗 19

21. 高挂红灯笼 瑞芳 19

22. 南国风光好 同贵 19

23. 南国水乡风景好 同贵 19

24. 江南年关 一陟................19

25. 和大哥 瑞芳..................20

26. 天仙子.同喜 重威.............20

文章..........................21

27. 花径..........................21

28. 如何拱猪 瑞芳................23

29. 如何拱猪 同贵................26

30. 如何拱猪 一陟 【英文】......30

31. 和睦的餐桌..................38

32. 中国珍珠元子................43

33. 致《……》作者.............44

遐想..........................45

34. 重庆：朝天门，解放碑，大礼堂....45

35.	引凤来巢	50
36.	寻冬地	53

论文 55

37.	劳技课机械制图的教学初探	55
38.	发表论文	60
39.	论文原稿	61
40.	论文英文翻译	64
41.	论文英文翻译原稿	70

备注 73

后语 74

歌曲

1. 壹. 徒步缙云

徒步缙云

作词：史瑞芳
作曲：史瑞芳

1=C 2/4 ♩=80

大钢琴 （ 2· 1 | 76 55 | 6 - ）‖: 553 553 | 13 54 | 3 - |
　　　　　　　　　　　　　　　　黑夜里，秋雨沥，并肩 向前 　行。

442 442 | 73 26 | 7 - | 6　1 | 7 | 6 56 |
公鸡啼，晨风拂， 泥泞 道难 　进。　　啊！　　　　缙　云　你
　　　　　　　　　　　　　　　　　　　啊！　　　　缙　云　你

7· 6 | 5 24 | 3 - | 66 11 | 22 33 | 16 56 | 0 0 :‖
多　么　隐　　秘，　　　饥渴 跋跎 探索 便服 融为 一体
多　么　柔　　美，　　　云腰 狮发 睡瞳 滴绿 飘逸 随心；

553 553 | 13 54 | 3 - | 442 442 | 73 26 | 7 - | 6 1 | 1 7 |
黑夜里，秋雨沥，并肩 向前 　行。 公鸡啼，晨风拂， 泥泞 道难 　进。 啊！　　缙

6 56 | 7· 6 | 5 24 | 3 - | 66 11 | 22 33 | 16 56 |
云　你　　多　么　温　　　馨，　　眼里 心中　赞叹 溢出　多少 甜美。

0 0 | 2· 1 | 76 55 | 6 - ‖
　　　 留　着　永远 不尽　的。

（1986年11月）

2. 《徒步缙云》创作背景

1986年11月带高89级1班学生郊游位于北碚区的缙云山狮子峰后,用了不到一小时的时间一气呵成。

周日凌晨一点,兵分7路徒步登顶,是从北碚区体育馆出发的。

周一读报课时间,恳请大家用诗词歌赋等形式抒发。当晚我家务完,工作毕,才想起明日我也必须有东西发表,提笔挥毫,自己逼自己,幸有灵感,留下此情!

3. 《徒步缙云》歌词

黑夜里,秋雨沥,并肩向前行。
公鸡啼,晨风拂,泥泞道难进。
啊!缙云你多么隐秘,饥渴摔跤,
探索征服,融为一体;
啊!缙云你多么柔美,云腰狮发,
腼腆滴绿,飘逸随心;
黑夜里,秋雨沥,并肩向前行。
公鸡啼,晨风拂,泥泞道难进。
啊!缙云你多么温馨,
眼里心中,赞叹溢出多少甜美,
盛着永远不尽的。

4. 《徒步缙云》原稿

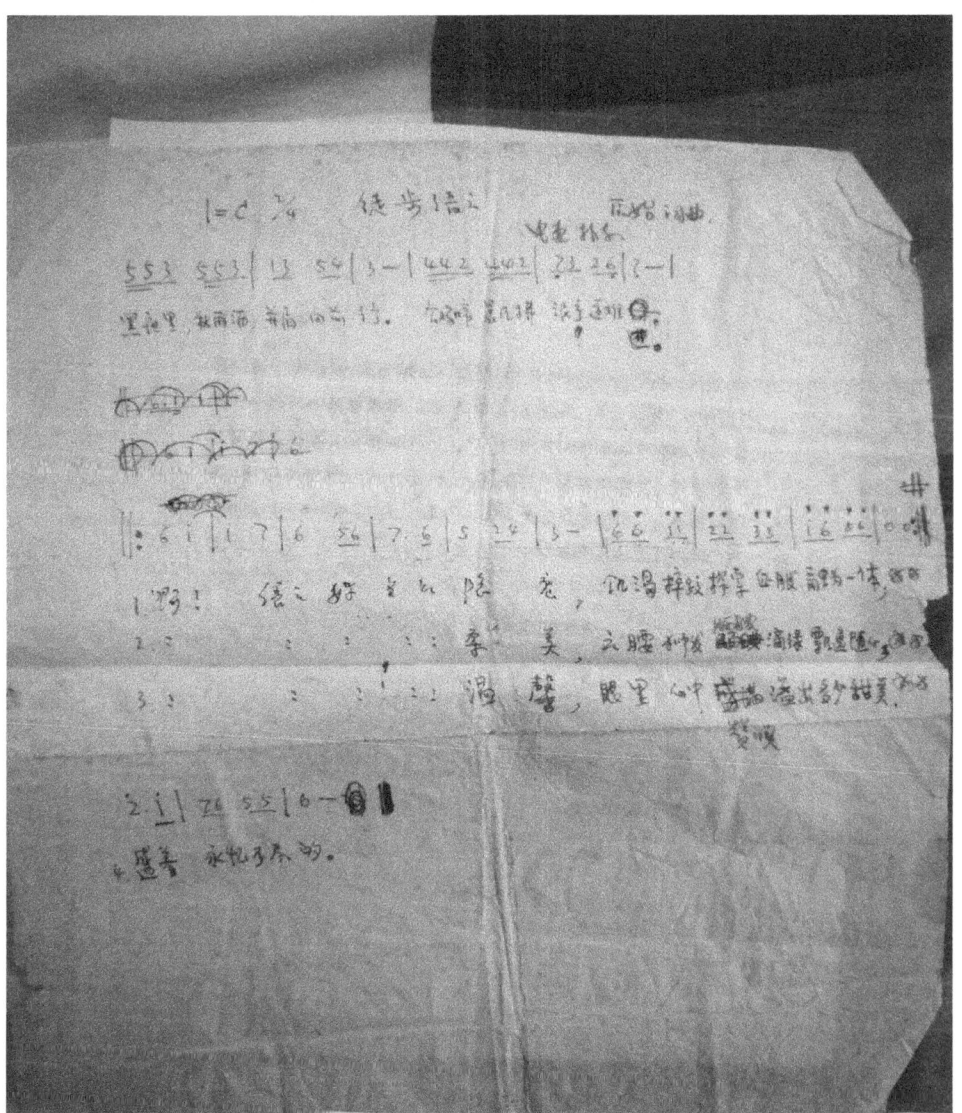

歌曲《徒步缙云》原稿。2005年5月以史瑞芳词曲唱在网上发表过。

5. 听《徒步缙云》有感 【中文】

妈妈，爸爸：

我们听了妈妈的《徒步缙云》，很不错。妈妈的风格和爸爸的明显不同。妈妈和爸爸的歌，词和曲都使人奋进，令人鼓舞。妈妈的顿音的运用给人一种悬念之感。简短而活泼的语言生动地表达了诗人登山时所发生的一切：山景的美丽，攀登的艰辛，征服的勇气以及登上峰顶的渴望。结尾却来了个"戛然而止"。从语法角度讲，最后一句看似不妥，我们似乎期待着在"永远不尽的"的后面还有点什么。从另一个角度讲，这也许正是诗人留给读者自己去想象的空间，因而也正是此歌高潮之所在。事实上，在"不尽的"之后什么都不写，让读者自己去充分地发挥想象，真正是达到了一种"不尽的"的效果。正如"余音绕梁，三日不绝"，让读者自己去寻找他们想要的"音"吧，每个人都会有自己不同的答案的。顺便问一句，云腰狮发，有没有什么典故？

多多保重

一陟

2005 年 5 月 31 日

6. 听《徒步缙云》有感 【中文原稿】

妈妈，爸爸：

我们听了妈妈的<徒步缙云>，很不错。妈妈的风格和爸爸的明显不同。妈妈和爸爸的歌，词和曲都使人奋进，令人鼓舞。妈妈的顿音的运用给人一种悬念之感。简短而活泼的语言生动地表达了诗人登山时所发生的一切：山景的美丽，攀登的艰辛，征服的勇气以及登上峰顶的渴望。结尾却来了个"戛然而止"。从语法角度讲，最后一句看似不妥，我们似乎期待着在"永远不尽的"的后面还有点什么。从另一个角度讲，这也许正是诗人留给读者自己去想象的空间，因而也正是此歌高潮之所在。事实上，在"不尽的"之后什么都不写，让读者自己去充分地发挥想象，真正是达到了一种"不尽的"的效果。正如"余音绕梁，三日不去"。让读者自己去寻找他们想要的"音"吧，每个人都会有自己不同的答案的。顺便问一句，云腰狮发，有没有什么典故？

多多保重

一陟

2005-5-31

7. 听《徒步缙云》有感 【英文】

Dear mom and dad,

    We listened to mom's "Tú Bù Jìn Yún (Climbing the Jinyun Mountains)". It's excellent! Mom definitely has a different style from dad's. In both mom's and dad's songs, the lyric and music have an urging and inspiring factor. Her use of staccato produced a sense of suspense. The use of short and brisk words vividly reflected what went through the poet's mind while scaling the mountains, the beauty of the mountains, the difficulties of climbing, the will to conquer them and the desire to get to the top. The ending is like "jiá rán ér zhǐ (an abrupt ending)". The last sentence seems to be grammatically improper. We are expecting something after "yǒng yuǎn bù jìn de (what will be ever endless)". On the other hand, this is probably the room the poet leaves readers to fill, and hence the climax of the song. The fact that there was nothing after "bù jìn de (endless)" lets readers to fill with whatever they imagine, thus producing the real effect of "endless", like "yú yīn rào liáng, sān rì bù jué (the music lingers on in the air for three days after the performance)". And here the readers are left to search for the "music" he or she would like, and each may come up with a different answer. By the way, what is "yún yāo shī

fā"? Does it have any "diǎn gù (classical allusions)"?
    Best Regards
    Yizhi
    2005-5-31

8. 听《徒步缙云》有感 【英文原稿】

Dear mom and daddy,

We listened to mom's "Tu Bu Jin Yun". It's excellent! Mom definitely has a different sytle from daddy's. Both mom's lyric and song have an urging and inspiring factor. Her use of staccato produced a sense of suspense. The use of short and brisk words vividly reflected what went through the poet's mind while climbing the mountain, the beauty of the mountain, the difficulties, the will to conquer them and the desire to get to the top. The ending is like "jia ran er zhi". It's not that the last sentence is grammatically improper. We were expecting something after "Yong Yuan bu Jing de". On the other hand, this is probably the room the poet leaves readers to fill, and hence the climax of the song. The fact that there was nothing after "endless" lets readers to fill whatever they like or think, thus producing the real effect of "endless", like "Yu2 Yin1 Rao4 Liang2, San1 Ri4 Bu2 Qu4". And here the readers are left to search for the "Yin1" he or she would like. And each may come up with a different answer. By the way, what is "Yun Yao Shi Fa"? Does it have any "Dian2 Gu4"?

Best Regards
Yizhi

9. 贰.树桩

英语Stump & 五绝律诗《树桩》

一陟贵芳

1=C 2/4　♩=132

(4̇ - | 3̇ - | 2̇ - | 2̇ 0) | 2 4 | 1̇ - | 7 6 | 6 0 |
　　　　　　　　　　　　　Don't pan- ic　stump
　　　　　　　　　　　　　树　桩　　心　　莫　慌

5 5 | 7 7 - | 6 6 6　5 | 5 0 | 7 7 | 6 - |
To your　res- cure　wa-ter will come　　New leaves will
有　水　会　　帮　　忙　　　　新　叶　知

5 5 | 4 | 4 0 | 4 4 4 | 5 - | 4 3 | 3 0 |
have their　day　　Green dresses will　　they don
天　日　　再　穿　青　　绿　裳

4̇ - | 3 - | 2̇ - | 2̇ 0 ‖
will　　they　　don
青　　　绿　　　裳

树 桩
儿歌

作词：史瑞芳
作曲：汪同贵

1=C 4/4　♩=140

(5 1̇ 5 1̇ | 5 7 1̇ - | 2̇ 4̇ 3̇ 2̇ | 1̇ - - -) | 5 1̇ 5 1̇ |
　　　　　　　　　　　　　　　　　　　　　　　树 桩 树 桩

5 7 1̇ - | 1̇ 1̇ 2̇ 3̇ | 5 - - - | 5 1̇ 5 1̇ | 5 7 1̇ - | 2̇ 4̇ 3̇ 2̇ |
莫心慌　　有水来帮　忙　　　树桩树桩　莫心慌　有水来帮

1̇ - - - | 5 7 1̇ - | 2̇ 3̇ 5 - | 5 1̇ 7 6 | 5 - - - | 5 7 1̇ - |
忙　　　抽　枝　　有天时　再穿绿衣裳　　　抽　枝

2̇ 3̇ 5 - | 2̇ 4̇ 3̇ 2̇ | 1̇ - - - | 5 7 1̇ - | 3 5 1̇ - | 2 - 4 - |
有天时　再穿绿衣裳　　　抽　枝　　有天时　再　穿

3 - 2 - | 1 - - | 1 - - 0 ‖
绿　衣　裳

10. 《树桩》创作背景：唱和地球树

　　2018年5月11日星期五，晚饭后，坐车去公园散步。走向波多马克河边的路上，一陟提议咏诗，见路边树桩倒在地上，"怎么样，就咏树桩"？ 两老人异口同声"好"！回家，晚8点我入睡。一觉醒来，拧开台灯，提笔就写了诗《树桩》，抬头看钟11:51 p.m.。

　　谢谢丈夫相伴，谢谢儿子提携，谢谢地球树。

史瑞芳

11. 《树桩》原稿

树桩莫心慌，
有水来和泥。
抽枝有天时，
再穿绿衣裳。

有一等　有天时一芽树
有天时——　有时节

2018/5/11　23:51　11:51 pm
日　一　二　三　四　五
5/6　7　8　9　10　11

桩

12. 咏《树桩》序 瑞芳

饭散天光亮，
坐车上公园。
走向波马河，
路边见树桩。

13. 咏《树桩》序 一陟

饭余天尚早，
散步上波江。
小路林中密，
蹊边见树桩。

14. 《树桩》律诗与英文翻译

《树桩》：	五绝律诗：	STUMP:
树桩莫心慌，	树桩心莫慌，	Don't panic stump,
有水来帮忙。	有水会帮忙。	To your rescue, water will come.
抽枝有天时，	新叶知天日，	New leaves will have their days,
再穿绿衣裳。	再穿青绿裳。	Green clothes will they don.

15. 《树桩》 儿歌 瑞芳

  树桩树桩莫心慌，有水来帮忙，
  树桩树桩莫心慌，有水来帮忙。
   抽枝有天时，再穿绿衣裳，
    抽枝有天时，再穿绿衣裳，
   抽枝有天时，再穿绿衣裳。

16. 《树桩》 七绝 一陟

    树倾留干小蹊边，
    立倒轮回不息眠。
    待到来年春草绿，
    问天再假一千年。

17. 《枯木树桩赞》 散文 同贵

　　在美国，走在林间路上，随处可见倒在路边的枯木，横七竖八，或连根翻倒，或拦腰折断，和一个个大大小小，高高低低，奇形怪状的树桩。

　　枯木树桩，给静静森林凭添了些许色彩，野性和苍凉。森林因她们更自然，更原始，更漂亮。

　　她们也曾生机勃勃，也曾枝繁叶茂，当初也许比同伴更高，更壮。她们也曾有过自己的辉煌。

　　如何形成这般景象，或因飓风，或遭雷劈。偌大一颗树，同在一片林，别的好好的，偏她倒下了，究其原因还是她自身的问题，或根基太浅，或疾病缠身，或时运不济。她们谁也不怪，认命了。认命，不折腾又何尝不是一种美德？

　　枯木树桩未必没有梦想，腐烂可以肥沃土壤，给别的伙伴提供营养。如果遇上能工巧匠，做成根雕，继续服务人类，再造辉煌。

　　树桩再发芽，枯木又逢春，也是有的。但那是侥幸，只可偶遇，不可奢望。

　　这美景我似曾相识，在九寨沟的海子里，在台湾阿里山上。

　　汪同贵随笔 2018 年 5 月 13 日 McLean, VA

18. 《树桩》 修改历程

树桩-史瑞芳：
树桩莫心慌，有水来帮忙。
仄平仄平平，仄仄平平平。
抽枝有天时，再穿绿衣裳。
平平仄平平，仄平仄平平。

Shù zhuāng mò xīn huāng,
yǒu shuǐ lái bāng máng.
Chōu zhī yǒu tiān shí,
zài chuān lǜ yī shang.

平起首句押韵式的要求格式：

平平仄仄平，仄仄仄平平。
仄仄平平仄，平平仄仄平。

树桩-五绝律诗：

树桩心莫慌，有水会帮忙。
仄平平仄平，仄仄仄平平。
新叶知天日，再穿青绿裳。
平仄平平仄，仄平平仄平。

Shù zhuāng xīn mò huāng,
yǒu shuǐ huì bāng máng.
Xīn yè zhī tiān rì,
zài chuān qīng lǜ shang.

首字不论,所以"新"字可平。

孤平拗救:

在"平平仄仄平"句式中,如果第一字用了仄,第三字必须用平。如上面下划线所示,为了尽可能保持原意,孤平拗救用了两次。

19. 叁.昆华赠围巾

昆华赠围巾

词：史瑞芳
曲：汪同贵

1=F 2/4
♩=80

(6̲3̲ 6̲7̲ | 1̲̇7̲ 6 | 3̲6̲ 2̲3̲ | 1̲7̲ 6) | 3 6 | 0̲2̲ 1̲2̲ | 3 5̲2̲ | 3 — |
　　　　　　　　　　　　　　　　　　　　　　　　　昆　华　　赠围　巾　赠围　巾

3 3 | 0̲1̲ 2̲3̲ | 6 6̲7̲6̲ | 3 — | 6 3 | 0̲1̲ 2̲3̲ | 2 0̲5̲ | 6̲7̲ 6 |
结　缘　五　十　年五十　年　　　战　友　无　言　语无言　语

6 7 | 0̲2̲ 3̲4̲ | 3 0̲6̲ | 3̲2̲ 3 | 2 3 | 2̲3̲ 5̲6̲ | 6 — | 6 0 |
心　盛　万　万　千万　万　千　心　盛　万　万　　千

‖: 3̲6̲ 2̲1̲2̲ | 3 — | 2̲2̲ 2̲2̲3̲ | 6 — | 6̲3̲ 1̲2̲3̲ | 2 — | 2̲3̲ 5̲6̲ | 6 :‖
昆华　赠围　巾　　结缘　五十　年　　战友　无言　语　　心盛　万万　千

3/4
3 — 6 | 2 — 1̲2̲ | 3 — — | (333) | 2 — 2 | 2 — 2̲3̲ | 6 — — | (666) |
昆　　华　赠　围　巾　　　　　　　结　缘　五　十　年

6 — 3 | 1 — 2̲3̲ | 2 — — | (222) | 2 — 3 | 5 — 6 | 6 — — | (666) ‖
战　友　无　言　语　　　　　　　心　　盛　万　万　千

20. 《昆华赠围巾》原诗

无题

昆华赠我俩,
结缘五十年。
战友无言语,
心盛万万千。

2018年10月8日于观音桥

和诗

21. 高挂红灯笼 瑞芳
    红灯笼引道，
    人在棹船中。
    水里鱼儿跃，
    桥桩立水东。

22. 南国风光好 同贵
    南国风光好，
    轻舟巷里行。
    红灯高处挂，
    更喜雪初晴。

23. 南国水乡风景好 同贵
    南国水乡风景好，
    小船悠荡巷中行。
    红灯高矮廊檐挂，
    游客心仪雨后晴。

24. 江南年关 一陟
    正月水城烟雨中，
    雪融犹白彩灯红。
    渔翁摇橹轻波里，
    年有年鱼望卖空。

25. 和大哥 瑞芳
　　　　泼猴眼珠转，
　　　　长幼一起涮。
　　　　王母笑靥嗔，
　　　　缘宫乐翻天。

幺妹：瑞芳
（缘宫：那天聚会的餐馆名含"缘"字）
2010年11月24日

26. 天仙子.同喜 重威
　　　祝贺一抒，育贤结婚
　　同喜声声持酒听，大陆宝岛喜联姻。云水相违半世纪，三通起，先占春。鸳鸯水暖两情深。
　　　远洋结褵大不易，云破月来花弄影。重关险度方到今，天涯路，不可轻。天意酬勤花满径。

　　幺妹，同贵：
喜知一抒，育贤在华盛顿完婚，立即电告仲芳，淑芳。山遥路远，不能前来祝贺，按成都乡规，又不能补礼，她们嘱我致意：同喜，同喜。父亲名下，孙辈从一抒这里圆满完成<收坛酒>，全家告慰，夜来吟成<天仙子>词一首，秀才人情纸半张，表意申忱，谨此致贺。
　　　　　　大哥 2008年7月21日

文章

27. 花径

旅游车开进庐山的中心——牯岭街,在花径公园的大门前停了下来。一走进公园,一个小圆亭——花径亭就跃入我的眼帘。走近一看,却象一圆形的"菜篮"加了个盖。亭太小游人不能进去,只能沿栏边往下观看。亭的底面镶嵌了一个条形的石碑,碑阴刻着两字:"花径",传说是白居易的手迹。不日毛主席看后说,不是他的手迹,古时花字的草头不是这样写的。两字涂成红色,但红色涂鸦,虽醒目,看起来却缺乏视觉意趣,因为每个人都靠着亭栏俯视,不合常用的平仰习惯,更不能祥说光感细节。往前再走几步,见一茅屋,导游曰:"白居易草堂,现为陈列室"。过一鱼背桥,只需上下两步,再行三步,拾级两梯,进入堂内,迎面玻璃框内装的不知何人书写的《大林寺桃花》篇:"人间四月芳菲尽,山寺桃花始盛开。长恨春归无觅处,不知转入此中来"。尺寸非条幅,有落款(字小),二十八个字如藤萝相连,写得随意流畅,非隶,非篆,非柳,非颜,整体飘逸,却不是草书张牙，圆而透迤。草堂坐北朝南，一门进，一排三间，它挂在中堂左隔扇上，权为正厅的中条。左室门前的左侧墙上又挂了一个玻璃框，此框较它尺寸稍大些，用小楷书《琵琶行》全文："浔阳江头夜送客……"。上午10时许的阳光正好打在正面和左侧，光线柔和，在密密麻麻的小楷对照下，那《桃花篇》更显妩媚。右室门前无字，左褒右贬，正符合文人政客古规，足见布置此室人的文化底蕴。只是现今的导游放到口边都不能信手拈来，实在不敢恭维。我想花径，就是观看桃花的路，只不过不便问起，无从查考。这是否是香炉峰，是否是大林寺，是否是移植来的，看完了，听完了，走过了，也是一笔糊涂帐，只是世人难得糊涂，不过也让我再也忘不了那桃花诗。虽看不见龙，却看见了龙眼睛。

2005 年 9 月 25 日 阴 农历 8 月 22 日

28. 如何拱猪 瑞芳

54张一副的扑克牌,六个人一起玩"拱猪",每一个人持有9张牌。九次出牌,一圈玩完。一个人全收齐,最高可得正4240(+4240)分:
4240=4x(100x2+100x2+330x2)
54张牌的组成:54=1+1+13x4
小鬼1张,大鬼1张;黑桃,方块,草花,红桃各13张(位),有相同的名和序。
13位的名,13位的序:2,3,4,5,6,7,8,9,10,J,Q,K,A,小鬼大鬼在拱猪时都归入"红桃序列"。
"红桃序列"中各位的负分(括弧中数字):
2(0),3(0),4(0),5(-10),6(-10),7(-10),8(-10),9(-10),10(-10),J(-20),Q(-30),K(-40),A(-50),小鬼(-60),大鬼(-70)。
红桃通常是负分,总的负分为-330分:
-330=-10x6-20-30-40-50-60-70
但是,如果某一牌手打某一圈牌时收齐("赢得")了所有红桃(包括大鬼小鬼),所有红桃变正330分。
收齐红桃序列又被卖红,是正330x2分。
拱猪时,黑桃Q是猪,没卖是负100(-100)分,被卖后是负200(-100x2)分。

但它在"一个人全收齐"中变成正100分,被卖后是正200(100x2)分。

方块J是羊,没卖是正100分,被卖后是正200(+100x2)分。

"一个人全收齐"中羊还是正100分,被卖后是正(100x2)分。

草花10是倒板。

一圈下来,只持这一张倒板,是正50(+50)分,被卖后是正(50x2)分。

一圈下来,持倒板又持其它有正负分的牌,则其它正负分的总和翻一倍,倒板被卖后,其它正负分的总和翻两倍。

"一个人全收齐"的概念:

一个牌手获得猪,羊,倒板,"红桃序列"(包括大鬼小鬼):

13+1+1=15("红桃序列")

18=1+1+1+(13+1+1)("红桃序列"加上猪,羊,倒板)

在九次出牌的过程中要收齐这18张牌,多么微妙啊!实力加运气。

拱猪可以少于6人,也可以多于6人。

例如5人玩,每个人持有10张牌,54张中拿走小鬼,大鬼,红桃2和3。

拱猪时,一圈下来,每个人头上或正分"+"或负分"-"或零分(0)。

几圈后，有人累计达到负 1000 分，就出局了（输了），这叫这头猪催肥了，这局结束。

重开一局，重新计分，接着玩"拱猪"。

"拱猪"开局第一圈指定第一个出牌是持有"黑桃 3"的人，出"黑桃 3"，就喊"拱猪"。

当然，也可以申明"黑桃 3"在我家，第一手不出"黑桃 3"。

这以后是上一圈耍完，得猪（黑桃 Q）的人出牌。

玩"拱猪"，先洗牌，发牌，收牌，确认完毕，只听"卖了"或者"甩了"，把那牌掷牌桌上公示，那就是"卖了"。

可卖的有：猪，羊，倒板，红桃 A（或者大鬼，如果没有被拿出去）。其它牌不可以卖。

卖红桃 A（或者大鬼，如果没有被拿出去）一张牌，叫"卖红"，是指红桃序列中的每一位都被卖了，也就是说所有红桃分值，不管正负，都要翻倍。

也有没人动声"卖"的时候。

2018 年 6 月 23 日 6:51 a.m.

29. 如何拱猪 同贵

拱猪是一种扑克牌游戏。

一副扑克牌54张。由红桃（红色）13张，黑桃（黑色）13张，方块（红色）13张，梅花（黑色）13张，大王/大鬼（红色），小王/小鬼（黑色）组成。

4人玩时只需要52张，一人13张，先抽出两张（大鬼小鬼）放一边不用。6人玩时54张全用上。

牌的大小顺序：最大是大鬼，小鬼，A（帽，尖），其次是K，然后依次是Q（框），J（钩），10，9，8，7，6，5，4，3，2。2点最小。

有分牌和无分牌以及算分的方法：
全部红桃牌都是有分牌，算负分，红桃帽负50，K负40，框负30，钩负20，其余的10点～5点这6张牌一张算负10分，红桃2，3，4这三张不算分。红桃的满分为负200。如果大鬼小鬼没有被拿出去，它们都算作红桃，小鬼算负60分，大鬼算负70分，这样红桃的满分为负330.

方块钩 J 叫羊，算正 100 分。
黑桃框 Q 叫猪，算负 100 分。
其余的牌是无分牌，不算分。
梅花 10 叫倒板（也叫变），谁得到倒板，谁的得分，无论正负，就翻一番（翻一倍）。

如果一个人把红桃包括 2，3，4（加上大鬼小鬼，如果没有被拿出去）全部收齐，红桃就由负分变成正分，满分为正 200 分（或 330 分）。如果谁把猪，羊，倒板，所有红桃全部都收齐，猪羊红桃全部算正分并乘以 2。400x2=800 或者 530x2-1060。

卖（亮牌），在摸牌的过程中和摸完牌后，出牌前，猪（黑桃 Q），羊（方块 J），倒板（梅花 10）都可以卖（把牌亮出来让大家知道在你家）。有红桃 A（或者大鬼，如果没有被拿出去）的，也可以卖红桃。凡是卖了的牌分数就翻倍计算：猪算负 200，羊正 200，大鬼负 140，小鬼负 120，红桃 A 负 100，红桃 K 负 80，红桃 Q60，红桃 J 负 40，红桃 5～10 点一张算负 20。红桃卖了全部收齐(包括 2，3，4)满分为正 400 或者 660。卖了的倒板翻一番后再翻一番(共 4 倍)，把卖了的猪羊倒板红桃全部收齐，则得正 3200(800x4=3200)或者 4240(1060x4=4240)。当然也可以不卖。根据自己牌的好坏自己决定卖不卖。卖过的牌不能在出同种牌的首轮出牌（除非该花色只有那张卖过的牌），但可以在别人出其它种牌的时候垫出去。

洗牌，玩牌前先把牌和转(即尽可能打乱原来的顺序并整理好)，倒扣着放桌子中间。摸牌（抓牌），4个人按反时针方向依次摸牌，一次取一张，摸到的牌只可以自己看，不要让别人看见。把所有牌摸完为止（每人摸到张数应该相同）。发牌，摸牌也可以由一人分发(发牌)。

出牌，首次由摸到黑桃3的先出牌(第一手必须出黑桃3，有些地区无此要求)。按反时针方向，依次一人一次出一张同种牌(即：先出牌人出红桃，其余人必须出红桃，先出牌人出的方块，其余人必须出方块，先出牌人出的黑桃，其余人必须出黑桃，先出牌人出的梅花，其余人必须出梅花)。如果没有同种牌，其它三种牌你就可以随便出，叫垫牌。四个人出完一轮牌后，看谁的牌大，谁就得该轮的全部分。牌的大小是在同种牌（正牌）中比较而言，如果没有同种牌而垫的其它牌不参与大小的比较。垫牌再大都小于正牌。

把有分牌捡到得分人面前面朝上摆着，其余的无分牌倒扣着放桌子中间。然后由牌大的先出牌。这样一轮一轮地直到把手里的牌全部出完。一局牌结束。以后的每一局就由上一局得猪的先出牌。

记分，一局牌结束后，把每人的得分用一张白纸记上。又重新开始第二局。一局完了又记分，把每人的得分累计。这样一局又一局玩下去。直到有人的累计得分满了负1000，他/她就输了（就是被喂肥了的猪🐷）。这一盘其他的人都赢了。

如果有人把猪，羊，倒板，所有红桃（包括大鬼小鬼），全部收齐，则这个人就赢了。其余三个人输。

如果三个人玩，把大鬼小鬼加进来，54张牌，刚好一人18张牌。大鬼算负70，小鬼算负60。如果6个人玩，把大鬼小鬼加进来，54张牌，刚好一人9张牌。大鬼算负70，小鬼算负60。6个人玩时也可以用两副牌。一个人18张。如果5个人玩，把大鬼小鬼和红桃2点3点这4张牌去掉，剩下50张牌，一人10张。也可以用两副牌，一个人20张。

30. 如何拱猪 一陟 【英文】

How to "Chase the Pig"

---- Yizhi

"Chasing the Pig"[1] is a very popular game in China and uses one deck of playing cards.

The Cards：

A standard deck of cards has 54 cards, including four suits: Spades, Hearts, Diamonds and Clubs. Suits are indicated by the suit sign on the corners of each card. A Spade is black and looks like a tree, a Heart is red and looks like a heart; a Diamond is red and looks like a diamond; and a Club is black and looks like a three-leaf grass. Each suit has thirteen cards: A (Ace), K (King), Q (Queen), J (Jack), 10, 9, 8, 7, 6, 5, 4, 3 and 2, with each card ranking higher than the card to its right. The two cards without any suit sign are Jokers, which are deemed to be Hearts when they are included in the deck. The red Joker is the Big Joker and the black Joker is the Small Joker. When applicable, the Big Joker ranks higher than the Small Joker, which, in turn, ranks higher than the Ace of Hearts.

---

[1] The Chinese term for this game is "拱猪" (pronounced as "gong zhu", literally meaning "to snout the pig [out of its pigsty]".

The Players:
The game is often played by four players. However, the game may also be played by three, five or six players. Both Jokers are removed from the deck when the game is played by four or five players. In addition, the 2 and 3 of Hearts are also removed from the deck when the game is played by five players. Consequently, each player will receive 18 cards in the event of three players, 13 cards in the event of four players, 10 cards in the event of five players and 9 cards in the event of six players.

Purpose of the Game:
Each player tries not to become "THE PIG" by gaining as many positive points as possible and avoiding as many negative points as possible. Any player who accumulates 1,000 or more negative points from one or more sets of play loses the whole game and becomes "THE PIG" of the game.

Points:
The Queen of Spades is the Pig and carries negative 100 points or negative 200 points when the Pig is Revealed (explained below), except that the negative points will turn positive in either case in the event of a Grand Slam (explained below). The Jack of Diamonds is the Sheep and always carries positive 100 points or positive 200 points when the Sheep is Revealed.

The Hearts carry negative points as follows, except that the negative points will turn positive in either case in the event of a Full House or a Grand Slam. Jokers, when applicable, are deemed to be Hearts.

Card	Un-Revealed	Revealed
Big Joker (when applicable)	-70	-140
Small Joker (when applicable)	-60	-120
Ace of Hearts	-50	-100
King of Hearts	-40	-80
Queen of Hearts	-30	-60
Jack of Hearts	-20	-40
10 of Hearts	-10	-20
9 of Hearts	-10	-20
8 of Hearts	-10	-20
7 of Hearts	-10	-20
6 of Hearts	-10	-20
5 of Hearts	-10	-20
4 of Hearts	0	0
3 of Hearts (when applicable)	0	0
2 of Hearts (when applicable)	0	0

The 10 of Clubs is the Multiplier and the recipient of the Multiplier will multiply all his or her points, positive or negative, by two or by four if the Multiplier is Revealed. However, if a player receives the Multiplier without the Pig, the Sheep or any of the Hearts, the player will receive positive 50 points or positive 100 points if the Multiplier is Revealed.

All the cards above under "Points" are "Relevant Cards".

The other cards do not carry any positive or negative points and are "Irrelevant Cards".

The Rule of Play:

The players sit around a table in a circle and designate any player as the dealer. The dealer shuffles the cards and places them in the center of the table, face down. The player to the left of the dealer "cuts" the deck (taking any number of cards on the top of the deck and putting them at the bottom of the deck to avoid any possible fraudulent dealing by the dealer). Then the dealer draws the first card from the top of the deck, the player to the right of the dealer draws the second card, and the next player draws the third card etc., until all the players draw all the cards counterclockwise. Each player should keep his or her cards confidential and it is illegal and immoral to see other players' cards. Each player should double check that he or she has received the correct number of cards as shown in

Section "The Players" above. It is desirable for each player to sort out the cards and hold them together in each suit in the hands to avoid inadvertent mistakes.

Initially, the player who holds the 3 of Spades is the opening lead. Such a player has the right to play the first card from any of his or her cards, which does not necessarily need to be the 3 of Spades. When the first card is played (placed in the center and shown to all players), the player to the right of the opening lead must play the next card and the other players continue to play their respective card in sequence counterclockwise until every player plays a card to complete that round. Each player must "follow suit" from the opening lead (playing a card from the same suit produced by the opening lead – the "Running Suit", if available). If no card of the Running Suit is available, a follower must "discard" any other card of his or her choice for that round. Such discarded card has no or lowest ranking and can never "win" a round. The player who plays the card with the highest ranking within the Running Suit "wins" that round, collecting all the Relevant Cards, placing them in his or her front, face-up for everyone to see. The Irrelevant Cards of that round are set aside in a pile. Such "winner" becomes the opening lead of the next round. All the players continue to play the rounds until all cards are played, ending that set of play. Each player will then count all the positive and negative points associated with the accumulated Relevant Cards in that set and record the outcome in a chart. If no player has become THE PIG at the end of such set of play, the players will continue to play the next set(s), accumulate the points from each set on the chart, until one or more player(s) has/have become THE PIG, who loses the game. Then the whole game is over and another game may begin anew.

Revelation:
Before a set of play begins, any player who holds the Pig, the Sheep, the Multiplier or the highest-ranking Hearts (the Ace of Hearts or the Big Joker, if applicable) may choose to "reveal" any or all of these cards by showing it or them to all the other players so that all players know who holds such revealed card(s). When revealed, the points normally attached to such card(s) (in the case of the highest-ranking Hearts, all other Hearts and deemed Hearts) will double and the Multiplier means a multiple of four instead of two.

A special rule for revelation is that, once a player reveals a card, such player is prohibited from playing such card for the first round of that particular suit, unless such player holds solely the revealed card in that suit but no other cards in the same suit at the beginning of a set of play.

Full House:
If a player collects all the available Hearts (including both Jokers, if applicable) in a set, all the negative points associated with the Hearts collected in that set become positive.

Grand Slam:
If a player collects each of the available Relevant Cards in a set, all the negative points associated with any of the Relevant Cards collected in that set become positive.

Rule Against Checking up the Dictionary:
No player shall fumble through the accumulated pile of Irrelevant Cards for information during any set of play, a practice called "checking up the dictionary".

Penalty for THE PIG:
1. The traditional penalty is for THE PIG to use his or her nose to "snout" a nicely-cut deck of face-up cards on the table until the Pig (Queen of Spades) is revealed.
2. A customary penalty is for THE PIG to crawl through under the playing table.
3. A sanitary penalty is to tape a sticker on the forehead or cheek of THE PIG, showing "I am THE PIG" or whatever fancies the players.

4. A sore PIG may hide the TV remote control of the player who has given THE PIG the Pig...

Invalidity of a Set of Play:
If at the last round of a set of play, one player has more or less than one single card, that set is declared invalid and should be replayed with a reshuffled deck. Alternatively, a penalty of negative 200 points is given to the player with fault because each player should make sure that he or she has the proper number of cards before the play of each set and gains or loses no cards wrongfully in the process.

31. 和睦的餐桌

绞肉机还在绞……
餐台上，一盘生鸡肉末，一盘生猪肉末，一盘生牛肉末……
一盘水果玉米粒，一盘高丽菜碎，一盘胡萝卜细碎，一盘芹菜可可……
一瓶醪糟（糯米发酵酿造），一瓶甜面酱（小麦发酵酿造），一瓶豆豉（黄豆发酵酿造），一瓶BBQ酱……
奶昔好香，喝一杯。饺子包好了两盘，还在包……
嘟嘟嘟，油烟机吼起来了。灶台上，油锅里，大火爆炒生牛肉末。包饺子的人喊："行了，快下甜面酱，调料……快翻炒……快装盘……锅里留点……洒开水，丢豆腐，勤翻炒，水干了，就装盘，不用再加水，芡粉，有酱……足够的味道……用切碎的辣豆瓣煎生牛肉末烧豆腐，还是一道著名的川菜……洗锅，炒鸡蛋西红柿和那几个菜。熬的汤随便喝，饭定量，炒鸡蛋西红柿不分盘……"。
晚餐就坐。先把西红柿汁全收进自己盘子里，然后跑冰箱开门东寻西找……盘里添这加那……叉子勺子一起翻堆，拿碗、装碗、扣碗，盘里一个"帽儿头"……拍照！拍照！手机画面里，红兮兮的是西红柿汁，肉末是点点，豆豉是可可，黄的是炒鸡蛋，红的是炒西红柿……树梢是芦笋尖，堆雪是醪糟，搭一片甜黄瓜，似"滑梯"……得意忘形。

早餐吃饺子，饺子有面，有咸味儿，还有肉和菜……早餐还吃水果，牛奶和鸡蛋。先喝100ml的凉白开水，再剥煮鸡蛋壳。"看！我剥的壳连成了一根，我剥得最好最快"！神气活现。多蓄汁去皮蒂。365天，有时只有把西红柿丢进开水锅里翻滚，漏勺捞出沥干水，放进干净的盘子里去皮去蒂，餐刀切块。

醪糟又叫米酒，还叫酒酿，戏称"酒饭"，是用糯米发酵酿成的。

醪糟家自做，甜味淡，酒味淡，晚饭合一勺生（不沾热）醪糟吃，最好是常在下午饮一小勺生醪糟汁，美白脸皮（个体差异）。

醪糟家（恒温20℃）自做，不费力，100个小时。只是酿米酒要求温度恰当，清洁度高，搭配精准。大中华超市甜曲一颗，配糯米375克，配37°C开水435克（分三次用，9/10+3/40+1/40=1）。

醪糟家（恒温20℃）自做，过程不复杂：2准备，6步，3要。

2 准备：
(2-1)曲粉：把甜曲饼辗成细末粉放进干净干燥的碗里。
(2-2)温瓶：瓶用买醪糟的瓶最好，用 40℃的开水涮几次瓶，把瓶和瓶盖放在干净的两支平放平行的筷子上。

6 步：
煮饭，饭降温，饭合曲，"凿井"又装瓶，瓶保温，瓶冷藏。
(6-1)煮饭：用电饭煲，糯米比等量粘米吸水少点，只是饭熟的灯一跳亮，就把糯米饭钵取出来。
(6-2)饭降温：（时间+9/10 水）。
两手四支筷子在糯米饭钵里快撬、快翻、慢洒水……
糯米饭降至 37℃左右(不锈钢钵不烫手)。
(6-3)饭合曲：在糯米饭钵里，少洒多翻……
甜曲粉和 37℃的糯米饭均匀混合是关键的一步，马虎不得，时间抓紧。
(6-4)"凿井"又装瓶：把以下 a，b，c，装入一个瓶里。
把钵里 37℃的糯米饭和甜曲粉的均匀混合物的全部(a)装入瓶，夯实。
饭高等于 2/3 瓶高。

然后在饭面中央"凿井"。就是把那四支筷子垂直插到瓶底。轻摇出一个中缝。把 1/40 水倒入甜曲粉空碗里，涮水全部(b)倒入中缝里。把 3/40 水倒入空钵里，涮水全部(c)倒入中缝里。最后，把四支筷子一支一支地轻摇慢抽，慢慢取出。保持井水面略低于饭面。拧紧瓶盖。

(6-5)瓶保温：干净浴巾裹紧瓶，外罩一个塑料袋，栓紧。瓶直立，瓶底平放烘干(衣)机里。24 小时(一整天)取出。500ml 的散热好的空瓶里，装满 100℃开水，拧紧盖，外罩一个塑料袋，栓紧。瓶直立，贴紧醪糟瓶，凉了(大约 5 小时)取出，关好烘干(衣)机门。

(6-6)瓶冷藏：瓶直立，瓶底平放在冰箱冷藏室里 72 小时(3 整天)。

<u>3 要：</u>
(3-1) 要把醪糟酿成的瓶保存在冰箱冷藏室里，保持瓶直立。
(3-2) 要用醪糟"醉"生肉。只需把醪糟生肉混合均匀(比例随意)，15 分钟多，碗里肉边一圈红，把吸水纸挨近红，碗底一点接触桌面，碗自然侧立，慢慢转动，多吸出点血水，这肉烧起好吃，油锅里生爆酱煎好吃，这肉加点芡粉混合均匀，油锅里炒起比较嫩……
(3-3) 要"脱瓶"又"转瓶"。醪糟酿成，粘连成一个整体。在玻璃瓶(上小下大)里，要

"脱瓶"又"转瓶"。在瓦缸(上大下小)里,要"脱缸"又"转缸"。在瓦罐(上大下小)里,要"脱罐"又"转罐"。见过"脱罐"又"转罐"。就是把一根干净的棍子垂直插入"凿井"里,轻用力,顺时针带动,那醪糟整体脱罐,在罐里顺时针转起来。神奇!

舀醪糟是在凿井里舀,井里的汁(米酒)舀干了,第二天又涨满了。日渐那醪糟整体垂直下陷,日渐那凿井缓慢扩大……不神奇,醪糟是用糯米发酵酿成的。

> 2018年7月7日 5:01 a.m.

32. 中国珍珠元子

内馅：	白砂糖，红豆沙（红豆煮烂，去皮留沙）。
外皮：	糯米粉，水，混合搓成团（球）。
珍珠：	糯米粒。

中国元宵节要吃"元"食品，预示团团圆圆。

今天是中国农历正月十五——元宵节。欢迎大家品尝珍珠元子。

元食品：	常见汤元，珍珠元子，麻元……
汤元：	内馅，外皮，开水锅里煮，吃热的。
珍珠元子：	汤元滚粘糯米粒，开水锅上架笼屉蒸，可热吃可凉吃。
麻元：	汤元滚粘芝麻粒，油锅里炸，可热吃可凉吃。

33. 致《……》作者

我俩是重庆市江北区红土地居民。川师（成都市）数学系66级毕业，川外俄语系66级毕业，重庆市字水中学退休人。十几年来，足落(703)地区，拜读大华府中文报上的文章，去听半杯清茶社……的讲座。

2017年4月，《陈九讲写作》在半杯清茶社。后在一张报纸的一张彩色照片上，面对讲台，最后一排右1右2两个老人就是我俩……

2018年7月20日星期五于北维

遐想

34. 重庆：朝天门，解放碑，大礼堂

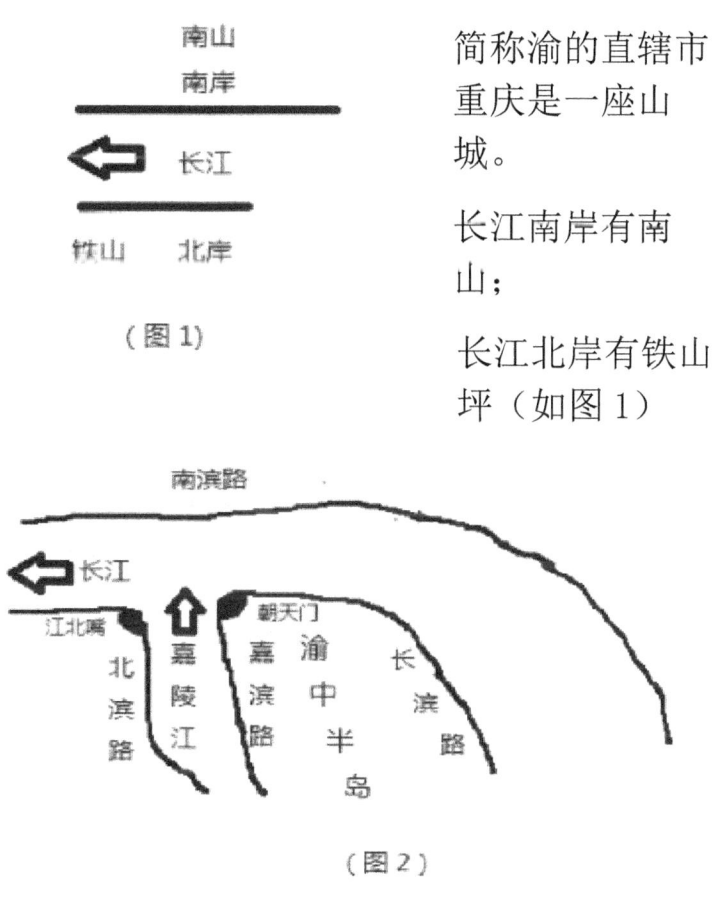

简称渝的直辖市重庆是一座山城。

长江南岸有南山；

长江北岸有铁山坪（如图1）

渝中半岛上有西山、枇杷山、鹅岭、浮图关、平顶山……

支流嘉陵江汇入长江后就形成了两江四岸的格局，还有突出的江北嘴、朝天门。

临江傍水的路叫滨路，在两江汇合口有名的南滨路、北滨路、嘉滨路、长滨路……（如图2）

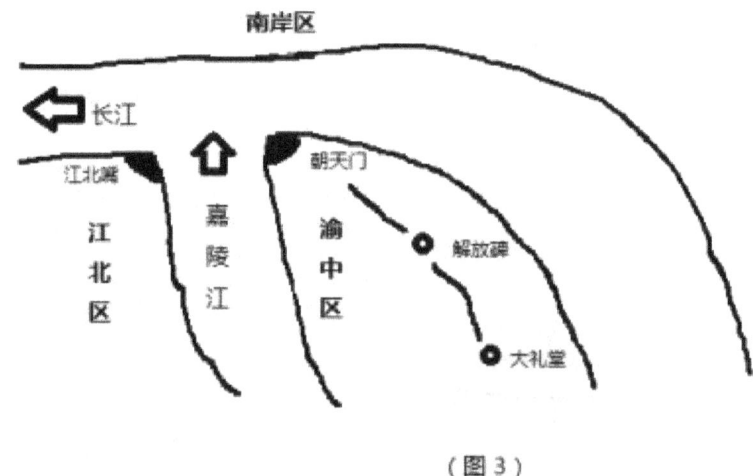

（图3）

外公外婆住南岸区；

爷爷奶奶住江北区；

朝天门、解放碑、大礼堂都在渝中区（如图3）

重庆很大，有四十来个区市县，还有一个两江新区。很多名胜古迹、人文自然景观，如长江三峡、奉节夔门、白帝城、张飞庙，忠县石宝寨、丰都鬼城、涪陵白鹤梁题刻、合川钓鱼城、潼南大佛、大足石刻、武隆仙女山、芙蓉洞、天生三桥、南川金佛山、綦江黑山谷……

在两江汇合处附近可看：江里行船；桥上跑车；空中溜索；缆车趴着。

缆车趴在小山坡上，停开了！那就是离朝天门最近的船码头——四码头。在朝天门附近还有十来个码头。无论上哪艘船，都得先到指定的船码头，沿梯坎下山坡，到江水边，过浮桥，上囤船，待船靠拢囤船时，人再登船。

坐船下行，重庆直达南京。中途可参观壮丽的长江山峡。空中溜索，就是看见空中有两个厢子来来往往，它们分别吊在两根绳子上，这两根绳子又连着长江两岸。那厢子里装的是人，白天几分钟就走一趟；晚上七点半开始，一趟十五分钟，供游客观赏重庆夜景的万家灯火。

游轮也是这样，白天让游客看两江四岸的美丽；晚上在船行中看万家灯火的重庆。

轮渡就是用船载人或车过江，所以这船又叫过河船，还叫摆渡船。

两江上有许多座桥。长江上有朝天门大桥、东水门大桥、长江大桥……；嘉陵江上有千厮门大桥、黄花园大桥、嘉陵江大桥……就近处可以看看南岸区的南温泉、南山植物园、大金鹰、老君洞、黄山抗战博物馆、文峰塔、加勒比水上乐园、一颗树观景台、垒山雕塑园、字水崖刻、洋人街、慈云寺、法国水兵营、南滨路上看朝天门、江北嘴、两江四岸、南坪商圈、步行街、国际会展中心、万达广场，江北区的江北嘴中央公园、大剧院、科技馆、观音桥商圈步行街、铁山坪森林公园、塔子山、江北区石子山体育公园、鸿恩寺森林公园……

渝中区的朝天门、解放碑、大礼堂、三峡博物馆、中山四路、红岩村、人民公园(在西山)、枇杷山公园、鹅岭公园、龙湖天街(斗味)、洪崖洞、湖广会馆、白象街、十八梯。凯旋路电梯连接上半城和下半城，较场口到储奇门，垂直上下连接，小商品市场（小什字）……

九龙坡区的黄桷坪涂鸦一条街、动物园、杨家坪商圈、步行街……

沙坪坝区的磁器口古镇、三峡广场、大学城、歌乐山红岩纪念馆……

渝北区的碧津公园、悦来会展中心、市中央公园、园博园、两江幸福广场(晚上有喷泉)……

北碚区的缙云山、北温泉、高坑岩、大磨滩……

大渡口区的工业博物馆(重钢旧址)……

巴南的物资集散中心（渝中区朝天门交易中心迁入）……

江津双福物资集散中心（江北区盘溪农贸市场迁入）……

壁山的观音塘湿地公园……

老重庆有朝天门、东水门（古迹尚存）、太平门、储奇门、金紫门、南纪门、通远门（不傍水，有通远门遗址公园，在七星岗车站附近）、临江门、千厮门……

克制冲动，服从安排，顾全大局，共同努力。

北京的中轴线：北端钟鼓楼，南端永定门，全长7.8公里。
故宫、天坛、景山、前门（正阳门）……都在中轴线上。

DC的中轴线：林肯纪念堂、国会山、方尖碑。

2015年7月1日

35. 引凤来巢

——迎接重庆至丰都的高速公路通车

民族的才是世界的

重庆市江丰股份有限公司 策划人史瑞芳

重庆市丰都县是长江上游难得的消费城市，地域简单，北岸、南岸、与长江成三条平行线。如图一所示。

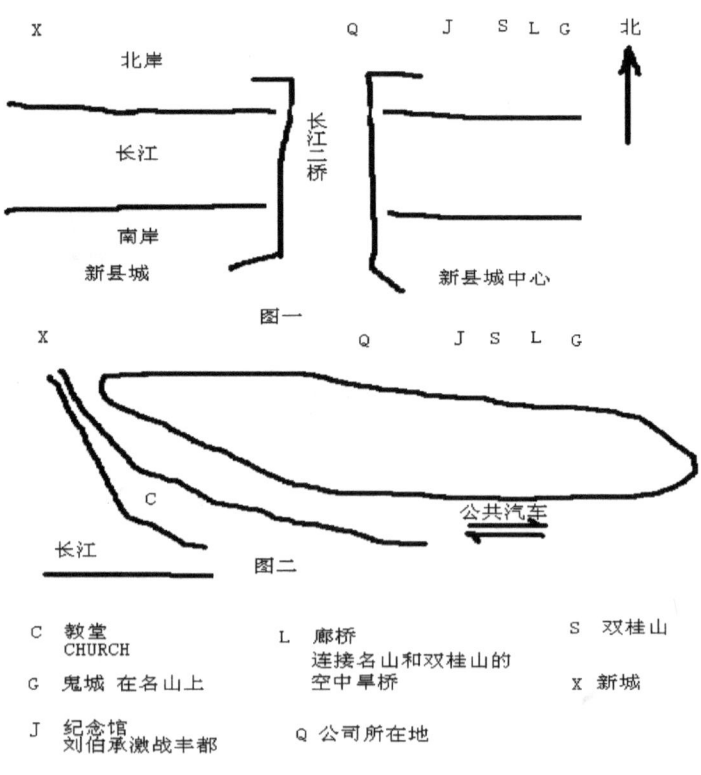

C 教堂 CHURCH
G 鬼城 在名山上
J 纪念馆 刘伯承激战丰都
L 廊桥 连接名山和双桂山的空中旱桥
Q 公司所在地
S 双桂山
X 新城

北岸有鬼城、双桂山、新城。南岸是新县城。新城有别于老城。丰都县城原在北岸，1871年长江涨洪水，曾迁行于此。现还有东门城墙留存。制高点的黄桷树的巨幅照片1999年在重庆市枇杷山博物馆亮相。新城江边还有一个新修不久的教堂(CHURCH)。新城如图二所示。

重庆市江丰股份有限公司在双桂山的山上修独立屋,山下修连栋屋,山边,公路旁修网络中心，保洁中心，物流配送中心，用工集训中心……在新城实现联网预定吃住。联络现有的歺馆，现有的宾馆，将现有的民间闲置房作家庭公寓，以此顺应重庆到丰都的高速公路通车的潮流,承接丰都长江二桥竣工后的繁荣。

在长江二桥新城桥头堡购房，开中歺馆，包旅游定点伙食，外卖等。引进麦当劳M，做烹饪定点实习地。在双桂山，新城，桥头堡三处都设小门店展示网购商品。

投资时局：

重庆市的丰都县，除了它的名山鬼城是世界上人、鬼、神之圣地外，长于农耕、肉牛养殖，政府推广养兔，故而今天交通都欠发达。花了八千万修长江大桥也是为将北岸的老县城迁往南岸落足，为长江175米水位蓄水的实现立下了汗马功劳。

即将完工的重庆至丰都的高速公路，为又一畅连东西大动脉的交通再修的长江二桥。

高速一通，农家乐休闲旅游成风，最佳接待地新城。

年底通车的渝利铁路途经涪陵，丰都，石柱。丰都县上了铁路网，鬼城游客激增。Welcome！

<u>旅游中乡</u>：

丰都肉牛片，海带汤

丰都兔丁，紫莱蛋花汤

丰都包面，长江鱼丸，东坡肉块

丰都榨莱肉丝汤

炒土豆丝，开胃时令泡莱

<u>畅想图</u>：

北岸的：东起鬼城，西止新城制高点黄桷树苗

新城的：教堂尖，东门城墙，制高点黄桷树苗

开发丰都，

建设丰都，

繁荣丰都。

2013 年 5 月 23 日

36. 寻冬地

道听途说，过冬去海南三亚最好，还有四川的西昌、米易、攀枝花、云南的昆明、广西的南宁。一路走了西昌、米易、攀枝花、昆明、南宁。西昌地比较平，米易有坡，攀枝花比重庆还山城。昆明、南宁都比较平。到西昌遇西伯利亚寒潮来袭，早晚冷，中午有太阳的时候就比较暖和，有点儿干燥。米易、攀枝花和西昌差不多。昆明有天日温1-19度。早上六点过出门呼出的气成白雾。南宁比昆明要暖和一些。过南宁的东兴关去越南玩了四天，参加的是南宁市内的广西海外旅行团。越南地较平，气候又比南宁好些。一路好吃的有：西昌邛海的鱼、火腿粗粮饭，再加一块钱，吃碗萝卜汤，这是第一次吃。还吃到了久违的川味回锅肉、米易的粑粑、攀枝花的盐边坨坨鸡、昆明的炒瓢儿白。南宁的盒饭，先点菜，再添一个人，再加三块钱的汤饭服务费。越南的汤煮细米线。一路看来。12月18日拜访了西昌月华水电厂。那天天冷风大，路遇公路秩序整顿。看了米易的人工湖，攀枝花境内的长江禁航区、三线建设博物馆、二滩水电站、昆明的西山、滇池、大观园、路南石林。参观了越南的总统府，越南下龙湾的"海上桂林"。

四川省西昌市凉山州人民政府：公民史瑞芳建议把西昌水电厂中的月华水电厂作为水电厂博物馆。

论文

37. 劳技课机械制图的教学初探

劳技课机械制图的教学初探
师生共同示范法

邮编： 400023 重庆字水中学 史瑞芳
提要： 劳技制图课要上得生动活泼，可运用师生共同示范法
关键词： 劳技、制图、示范

劳动技术教育课是普通中学的一门必修课。其中，高中一年级以机械制图为主。

机械制图初步介绍机械制图的基本知识，正投影分面图法和轴测投影法。基本内容包括六视图（主视图、俯视图、左视图、右视图、仰视图、后视图）、剖视图、剖面图、常用零件图、三种轴测投影图（正等轴测图，简称正等测。正二等轴测图，简称正二测。斜二等测视图，简称斜二测）的识读和绘制以及简单配图的识读。

一个学生经过一年（至多 $2\times2\times17=68$ 节课）的学习，要达到对着一个简单的零件或它的木模，画出它的三视图（主视图、俯视图、左视图），它的两种轴测图（正等测和斜二

测），相应的就是《立体几何》中的两种直观图，时间太短，安排必须十分紧凑。

一个初三毕业生，鉴于省会考对图画要求不高，升上高一的学生，画图能力差，绘图工具少，而且头脑中已经积累了多年的劳技课不过如此的印象。如何提高学生的学习兴趣？如何让学生主动，积极地参与课堂活动？如何在学生动手中使他们最大限度地受益？

如果采用老师在黑板上画一笔，学生在下面跟画一笔的老办法会枯燥无效，事倍功半，体育课请一个学生作动作示范的形式启发了我，就是请学生教学生。

下面谈谈师生共同完成示范的具体做法和效果。

每一节课，给每个学生发空白的绘图纸一张。印发的资料课内用一点发一点，不集中把所有一学期内用的资料发给学生保管。否则，学生不经意丢失或上课时忘了带来，一个班只要有十几个学生没有了图纸样，该课堂就难以有较好的效果。每一节课要求学生在绘图纸上首先画好A4（横式）的图框，取准图幅。然后要求学生利用该纸的废边角地带作好课堂笔记（学生没有教材），教师登记评优。学生在图框内画图，至多一周内完成，并上交教师审核。

学生按所发资料，在座位上个人独立完成自己的绘图，可以参考黑板上的板演画法，规定抄板书画法，鼓励提出修改意见。课堂内一名学生在黑板上画框样，教师口授要领，并与之磋商，尊重其总体规划，共同完成示范。由学生甲回答别的学生的提问，这种学生回答学生问题，语言习惯接近，不拘束，极易沟通。

学生乙板书画法，照抄教案。教材中大多数只有一个图，教师备课时必须根据学生画图的实际能力。已经学过了的初中《几何》的画法语言，配合高中一年级的《立体几何》的内容、进度，还得提前介绍高中二年级才能学习的《平面解析几何》涉及的部分内容。土观地拟定画法，充分地运用点集；用交集、并集等符号和语言，表述机械图样的画图过程，供学生参考。

学生丙在讲台附近放置的小平板上完成绘图，享用学校提供的一套正规绘图工具。教师解剖"麻雀"，发现他（她）的问题，再下访其他同学，找出通病，即时讲评，马上纠正。

这样，课堂内学生积极主动，象自行车队，各驶各的，在同一条大道上，朝着同一个目的地奔去。学生进行创造性劳动时人人处于兴奋状态。瞧，学生举着作品的得意相，教师高兴，与远看画图效果的板画者交流，教师快活。

堂内学生板画，速度较快，节省时间，同时学生得到锻炼。高一学生已不愿主动上讲台，开始教师可按序点名，或按学号，或按座次派定。经过一段时间的摸索，一批尖子自然形成，后期图样难度很大，可集中一个或几个能干学生板演画图。经观察，这些学生大多到高二时开始专攻美术专业。可见，这种新教学法可获得良好效果。

个人简历：
史瑞芳 女 1944 年 3 月 29 日生
中学一级教师
四川师范大学 66 级数学系毕业，现为重庆市字水中学教师

参考书目：
1.《制图》（修订本）
中学劳动技术课本 7-5428-0066-3
上海科技教育出版社 90.6 第 2 版 91.6 第 6 次印刷
2.《中学教师继续教育问题》
张家祥 金锵编著 7-81035-144-3
杭州大学出版社 91.9 第 1 版 96.1 第 3 次印刷
3《立体几何》（必修）
《几何》

《平面解析几何》
人民教育出版社 90 年版
4《机械制图》
中华人民共和国国家标准
GB 4457-4460-84
GB 131-83
中国标准出版社 84.9 第 1 版 85.3 第 1 次印刷
书号：15169.1-2676

38. 发表论文

此稿载入 ISBN 7-80607-368-X《中国教师优秀论文集成》发表。

39. 论文原稿

劳技课　机械制图的教学初探
师生共同示范法

邮编：400023　重庆字水中学史瑞芳
提要：劳技制图课要上得生动活泼，可运用师生共同示范法。
关键词：劳技、制图、示范

　　劳动技术教育课是普通中学的一门必修课，其中，高中一年级以机械制图为主。
　　机械制图初步介绍机械制图的基本知识，正投影分面图法和轴测投影法。基本内容包括六视图（主视图、俯视图、左视图、右视图、仰视图、后视图）剖视图、剖面图、常用零件图、三种轴测投影图（正等轴测图，简称正等测。正二等轴测图，简称正二测，斜二等测视图，简称斜二测。）的识读和绘制以及简单配图的识读。
　　一个学生经过一年（至多 2×2×17=68 节课）的学习，要达到对着一个简单的零件或它的木模，画出它的三视图（主视图、俯视图、左视图），它的两种轴测图（正等测和斜二测）。相应的就是《立体几何》中的两种直观图，时间太短，安排必须十分紧凑。
　　一个初三毕业生，鉴于省会考对图画要求不高，升上高一的学生，画图能力差，绘图工具少，而且头脑中已经积累了多年的劳技课不过如此的印象。如何提高学生的学习兴趣？如何让学生主动，积极地参与课堂活动？如何在学生动手中使他们最大限度地受益？
　　如果采用老师在黑板上画一笔，学生在下面跟画一笔的老办法会枯燥无效，事倍功办，体育课请一个学生作动作示范的形式启发了我，就是请学生教学生。
　　下面谈谈师生共同完成示范的具体做法和效果。
　　每一节课，给每个学生发空白的绘图纸一张，印发的资料课内用一点发一点，不集中把所有一期内用的资料发给学生保管。否则，学生不经意丢失或上课时忘了带来，一个班只要有十几个学生没有了图纸样，该课堂就难以有较好的效果。每一节课要求学生在绘图纸上首先画好 A4（横式）的图框，取准图幅。然后要求学生利用该纸的废边角地带做好课堂笔记（学生没有教材），教师登记评优，学生在图框内画图，至多一周内完成，并上交教师审核。
　　学生按所发资料，在座位上个人独立完成自己的绘图，可以参考黑板上的板演画法，课堂抄板书画法，鼓励提出修改意见。课堂内一名学生在黑板上画框样，教师口授要领，并与之磋商，尊重其总体规划，共同完成示范。由甲回答别的学生的 提问，这种学生回答学生问题，语言习惯接近，不拘束，及易沟通。

学生乙板书画法，照抄教案，教材中大多数只有一个图，教师备课时必须根据学生画图的实际能力。已经许学过了的初中《几何》的画法语言，配合高中一年级的《立体几何》的内容、进度，还得提前介绍高中二年级才能学习的《平面解析几何》涉及的部分内容，主观地拟定画法，充分地运用点集：用交集、并集等符号和语言，表述机械图样的画图过程，供学生参考。

学生丙在讲台附近放置的小平板上完成绘图，享用学校提供的一套正规绘图工具。教师解剖"麻雀"，发现他（她）的问题，再下访其他同学，找出通病，即时讲评，马上纠正。

这样，课堂内学生积极主动，象自行车队，各使各的，在同一条大道上，朝着同一个目的地奔去。学生进行创造性劳动，时人人处于兴奋状态，瞧学生举着作品的得意像，教师高兴，与远看画图效果的板画者交流，教师快活。

堂内学生板画，速度较快，节省时间，同时学生得到锻炼。高一学生已不愿主动上讲台，开始教师可按序点名，或按学号，或按座次派定。经过一段时间的摸索，一批尖子自然形成，后期图样难度很大，可集中一个或几个能干学生板演画图。经观察，这些学生大多到高二时开始专攻美术专业。可见，这种新教学法可获得良好效果。

个人简历：
史瑞芳　女　1944年3月29日生　　中学一级教师
四川师范大学66级数学系毕业，现为重庆市字水中学教师

参考书目：

1. 《制图》 （修订本）

    中学劳动技术课本 7-5428-0066-3

    上海科技教育出版社 90.6 第 2 版 91.6 第 6 次印刷

2. 《中学教师继续教育问题》

    张家祥 金锵 编者 7-81035-144-3/, 054

    杭州大学出版社 91.9 第 1 版 96.1 第 3 次印刷

3. 《立体几何》 （必修）

    《几何》

    《平面解析几何》

    人民教育出版社 90 年版

4. 《机械制图》

    中华人民共和国 国家标准

    GB 4457-4460-84

    GB 131-83

    中国标准出版社 84.9 第 1 版 85.3 第 1 次印刷

    书号：15169.1-2676

40. 论文英文翻译

CREATIVE TEACHING METHOD FOR MECHANICAL DRAWING
DEMONSTRATION BY BOTH TEACHER AND STUDENTS

LABOR SKILL COURSE

SHI RUIFANG
CHONGQING ZISHUI MIDDLE SCHOOL

SYNOPSIS: To make the Mechanical Drawing class vivid and intriguing, teachers may engage students in demonstration.

KEY WORDS: Labor skills; Mechanical drawing: Demonstration

The Labor Skill Courses are compulsory in high schools. Freshmen are required to take Mechanical Drawing.

The course consists of introduction to mechanical drawing, orthographic projection and pictorial projection. The major content includes six-view drawings: front (elevation) view, top (plan) view, left view, right view, upward view and back view. Cut-open view, section view and parts view are also covered. In pictorial projection, isometric, dimetric and oblique axonometric methods are introduced. The course objective is to enable students to understand and draft these views and their auxiliary views.

After one academic year (68 meetings at most including biweekly sessions for seventeen weeks of two semesters), a student should be able to draw the three views (namely front, top and left views), isometric and dimetric views of a simple part or its wooden model. These views correspond to the actual drawings in Solid Geometry. As a result, the class must be arranged neatly to cover all these topics.

Since little is required to develop students' drawing ability by the Provincial High School Entrance Examination, the freshmen are poor in drawing pictures and are far from familiar with the drawing tools. To make matter worse, most of them have developed an idea that labor skill courses are nothing but supplementary. Therefore, how to raise their interest and ensure active class participation becomes a big challenge. The theme of this thesis is to bring maximum benefit to the students by engaging them in the actual drawing.

The traditional way by which teachers draw on blackboard and students copy on their notebooks proves to be tedious and boring. Students don't learn as much as their time and energy deserve. I was enlightened by a practice in Physical Education, where an instructor asks a student to demonstrate the actions under discussion. Students teaching students may have extra effect.

In the following paragraphs, I will address the specific method and effect of a demonstration completed by both teacher and students.

At the beginning of each session, a student will receive a piece of blank drawing paper. The teaching materials should be distributed at each session. If the course packets for the whole semester have been given to students altogether, they tend to either lose them or forget to take them to class. Should a quarter of the students come to class without the samples, the teacher may find it very difficult to have a successful session.

At each class, the students first map a frame on an A4 paper (horizontal) and decide on its dimension. They will use the margins to take notes, for they do not have textbooks. The teacher will comment on their notes. Students are required to finish their own drawings in a week at most and submit them to the teacher for review.

According to the distributed materials, the students accomplish their drawings independently at their desk. The teacher can either ask them to exactly copy the drawing on the blackboard or just use it as a reference. They are encouraged to offer comments.

One student will be selected to chart the drawings on the blackboard. The teacher tells him or her the gist of it and consults with the student, who enjoys the freedom to choose the specific way to accomplish the task. With the help of the teacher, the student will complete the demonstration. Meanwhile, the student will also answer any questions from the class. It is much easier for students to communicate with themselves in their own language.

    Another student is chosen to duplicate the standard drawings from the Teachers' Manual onto the blackboard. In most cases, there is only one standard drawing for each problem. The teacher should account for the actual drawing ability of the students. He or she should use the language of Geometry, which has already been covered in the middle school, arrange the class in lockstep with Solid Geometry, a compulsory course for freshmen in high school, and introduce parts of Plane Analytic Geometry for their next year's study. The drawing process can be shown by properly using concepts like *point sect*, *intersection*, and *union*, or symbols like $\cap$, $\cup$, $\subset$ and $\in$.

    Still another student, facilitated with a whole set of standard drawing tools provided by the school, is asked to complete the drawing on a small board beside the podium. The teacher follows him or her closely and finds out any problems with the process. Meanwhile the teacher walks around the class to locate common errors and correct them accordingly.

In this way, the students are active and enthusiastic in class, moving towards their own direction like cyclists on the road. It is very exciting for students to have such creative work. The teacher is gratified by looking at the elated students relishing their own work. It is also a great pleasure to communicate with the students working in the front.

Students tend to do a quicker job when chosen to work on the blackboard. This saves time and sharpens his or her skills. Since freshmen are reluctant to volunteer to come to the podium, the teacher can cold call them according to student ID or sitting order at the beginning. After some time, several students will stand out. For the latter half of the course, there are some complicated drawings. The teacher can rely on these students to show others on the blackboard. It is my observation that most of such students begin to focus on fine arts when they become sophomores.

After much practice, the creative teaching method has produced excellent result.

Bibliography
1. Zhang Jiaxiang and Jin Qiang. *Problems in the Improvement of Middle School Teachers*. Hangzhou: Hangzhou University Publishing House, 1991.

2. *Book of Labor Skill in Middle School: Drawing 2nd ed*, Shanghai: Science, Technology and Education Publishing House, 1990.
3. *Geometry*. Beijing: People's Education Publishing House, 1990.
4. *Mechanical Drawing*, Beijing: China Standard Publishing House, 1984.
5. *Plane Analytical Geometry*. Beijing: People's Education Publishing House, 1990.
6. *Solid Geometry*. Beijing: People's Education Publishing House, 1990

All English counterparts of Mechanical Drawing terminology are from the Ninth Volume, Encyclopedia Americana and the Fifteenth Volume, Collier's Encyclopedia in City Library of New York.

41. 论文英文翻译原稿

CREATIVE TEACHING METHOD FOR MECHANICAL DRAWING
DEMONSTRATION BY BOTH TEACHER AND STUDENTS
LABOR SKILL COURSE

SHI, RUIFANG
CHONGQING ZHISHUI MIDDLE SCHOOL

SYNOPSIS: To make the Mechanical Drawing class vivid and intriguing, teachers may engage students in demonstration.

KEY WORDS: Labor skills; Mechanical drawing; Demonstration

The Labor Skill Courses are compulsory in high schools. Freshmen are required to take Mechanical Drawing.

The course consists of introduction to mechanical drawing, orthographic projection and pictorial projection. The major content includes six-view drawings: front (elevation) view, top (plan) view, left view, right view, upward view and back view. Cut-open view, section view and parts view are also covered. In pictorial projection, isometric, dimetric and oblique axonometric methods are introduced. The course objective is to enable students to understand and draft these views and their auxiliary views.

After one academic year (68 meetings at most including biweekly sessions for seventeen weeks of two semesters), a student should be able to draw the three views (namely front, top, and left views), isometric and dimetric views of a simple part or its wooden model. These views correspond to the actual drawings in Solid Geometry. As a result, the class must be arranged neatly to cover all these topics.

Since little is required to develop students' drawing ability by the Provincial High School Entrance Examination, the freshmen are poor in drawing pictures and are far from familiar with the drawing tools. To make matter worse, most of them have developed an idea that labor skill courses are nothing but supplementary. Therefore, how to raise their interest and ensure active class participation becomes a big challenge. The theme of this thesis is to bring maximum benefit to the students by engaging them in the actual drawing.

The traditional way by which teachers draw on blackboard and students copy on their notebooks proves to be tedious and boring. Students don't learn as much as their time and energy deserve. I was enlightened by a practice in Physical Education, where instructor asks a student to demonstrate the actions under discussion. Students teaching students may have extra effect.

In the following paragraphs, I will address the specific method and effect of a demonstration completed by both teacher and students.

At the beginning of each session, a student will receive a piece of blank drawing paper. The teaching materials should be distributed at each of every session. If the course packets have been given to students once and for all, they tend to either lose them or forget to take them to

1

class. Should a quarter of the students come to class without the samples, the teacher may find it very difficult to have a successful session.

At each class, the students first map a frame on an A4 paper (horizontal) and decide on its dimension. They will use the margins to take notes, for they do not have textbooks. The teacher will comment on their notes. Students are required to finish their own drawings in a week at most and submit them to the teacher for examination.

According to the distributed materials, the students accomplish their drawings independently at their desk. The teacher can either ask them to exactly copy the drawing on the blackboard or just use it as a reference. They are encouraged to offer comments.

One student will be singled out to chart the drawings on the blackboard. The teacher tells him or her the gist of it and consults with the student, who enjoys the freedom to choose the specific way to accomplish the task. With the help of the teacher, the student will complete the demonstration. Meanwhile, the student will also answer any questions from the class. It's much easier for students to communicate with themselves in their own language.

Another student is chosen to duplicate the standard drawings from the Teachers' Manual onto the blackboard. In most cases, there is only one standard drawing for each problem. The teacher should account for the actual drawing ability of the students. He or she should use the language of Geometry, which has already been covered in the secondary school, arrange the class in lockstep with Solid Geometry, a compulsory course for freshmen, and introduce parts of Plane Analytic Geometry for their next year's study. The drawing process can be shown by properly using concepts like *point sect, intersection*, and *union*, or symbols like $\cap, \cup, \subset$, and $\in$.

Still another student, facilitated with a whole set of standard drawing tools provided by the school, is asked to complete the drawing on a small board beside the podium. The teacher follows him or her closely and finds out any problems with the process. Meanwhile the teacher walks around the class to locate common errors and correct them accordingly.

In this way, the students are active and enthusiastic in class, moving towards their own direction like cyclists on the road. It's very exciting for students to have such creative work. The teacher is gratified by looking at the elated students relishing their own work. It's also a great pleasure to communicate with the students working in the front.

Students tend to do a quicker job when chosen to work on the blackboard. This saves time and sharpens his or her skills. Since freshmen are reluctant to volunteer to come to the podium, the teacher can cold call them according to student ID or sitting order at the beginning. After some time, several students will stand out. For the latter half of the course, there are some complicated drawings. The teacher can rely on these students to show others on the blackboard. It is my observation that most of such students begin to focus on fine arts when they become sophomores.

After much practice, the creative teaching method has produced excellent result.

Bibliography
1. Zhang Jiaxiang and Jin Qiang. *Problems in the Improvement of Middle School Teachers*. Hangzhou: Hangzhou University Publishing House, 1991.
2. *Book of Labor Skill in Middle School: Drawing* 2nd ed., Shanghai: Science, Technology and Education Publishing House, 1990.
3. *Geometry*. Beijing: People's Education Publishing House, 1990.
4. *Mechanical Drawing*. Beijing: China Standard Publishing House, 1984.
5. *Plane Analytical Geometry*. Beijing: People's Education Publishing House, 1990.
6. *Solid Geometry*. Beijing: People's Education Publishing House, 1990

All English counterparts of Mechanical Drawing terminology are from the Ninth Volume, Encyclopedia Americana and the Fifteenth Volume, Collier's Encyclopedia in City Library of New York.

备注

A. 歌曲《树桩》，《拱猪》，《和睦的餐桌》2018年7月20日投《……》作者邮箱，投《新世界时报》，投《侨报周末大华府地区周末版》。

B. 《引凤来巢》邮寄重庆市人民政府和丰都县人民政府。

后语

唱和：形式多样，人数不定，体裁无限。

一种：如：
"……唱山歌嘞，这边唱来那边和……"
《刘三姐》1961年发行的电影。

一种：联诗，如：
"……　凤姐道：一夜北风紧，
　　　　李纨道：开门雪尚飘。入泥怜洁白，
　　　　香菱道：匝地惜琼瑶。有意荣枯草，
　　　　　　　　……"
《红楼梦》1997年人民文学出版社出版第50回
--芦雪庭争联即景诗　暖香坞雅制春灯谜

一种：联诗作序，联诗湮没，序尚存。如：
"……落霞与孤鹜齐飞，秋水共长天一
色……"
唐·王勃《滕王阁序》（即《滕王阁诗序》）
滕王阁：江西省南昌市第29次重新修建。
在秋水公园一处，观看赣江对岸的滕王阁，天
上人间。

　　　　　　　　　　　　史瑞芳
　　　　　　　　　　　2020年6月3日于重庆

www.ingramcontent.com/pod-product-compliance
Lightning Source LLC
Chambersburg PA
CBHW071330040426
42444CB00009B/2126